MW01234776

My 1st BASEBALL BABY BOOK

Love This Book?

CHECK OUT MORE PRODUCTS BY
SCANNING THIS QR CODE!

SCAN ME

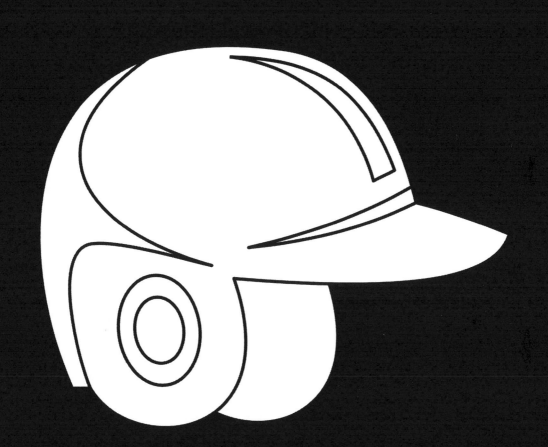

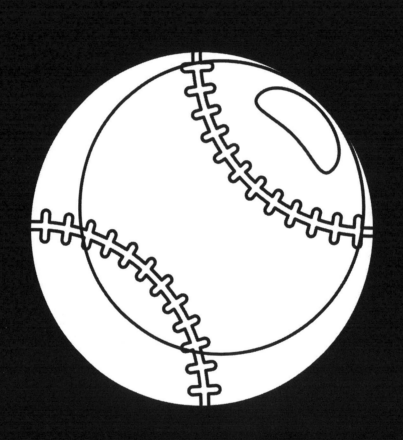

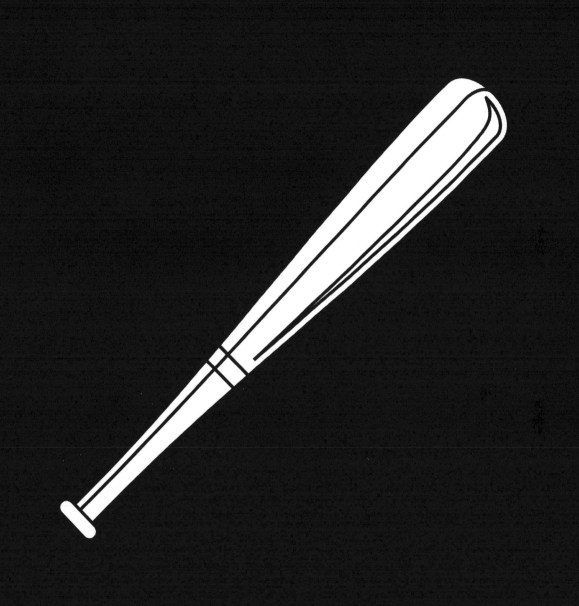

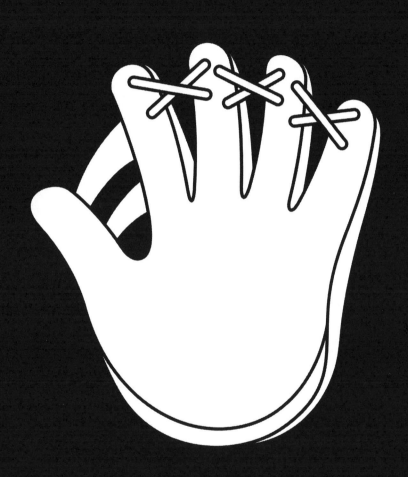

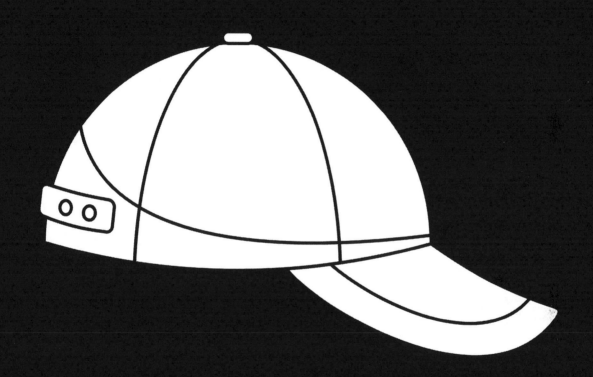

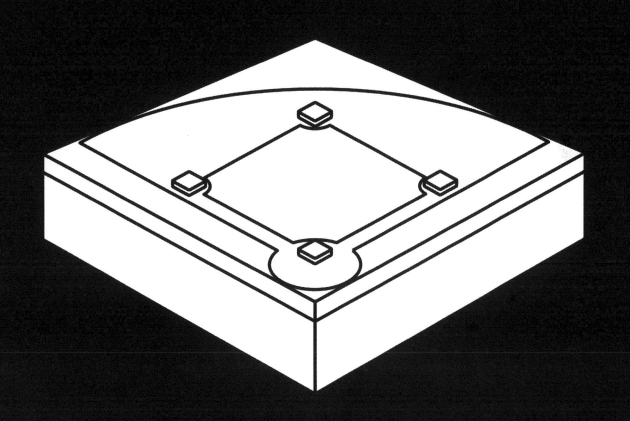

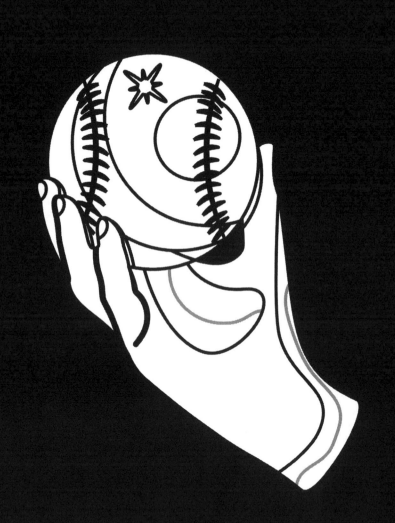

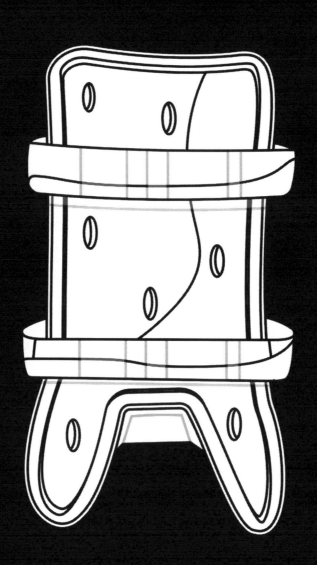

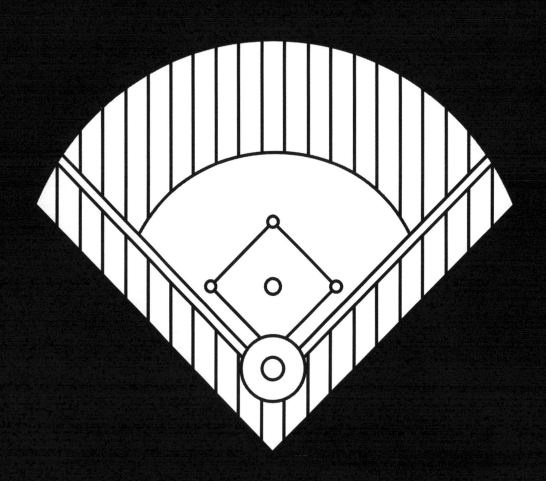

Thank you for getting my book!

If you find this baseball baby book fun and useful.
I would be very grateful if you posted a review on Amazon!
Thanks to your review. I can improve myself and it will help me
create better books.

If you would like to leave a review.
just head on over to this book's Amazon page and click
"Write a customer review".

Thank you. your support matters!

I invite you to visit my author's page
where you can find other interesting products.

Abbigail Lillie Publishing

Made in the USA
Las Vegas, NV
02 July 2024

91767560R00015